Spiritual England s
amusing, inspiring

Psychic News said: "the author challenges you to discover the meaning of dowsing"

Indie Shaman Magazine said "advice on how to dowse with a pendulum plus some ideas on things you can dowse for...written in an informal style"

Genuine Reader Review "An enjoyable introduction to pendulum dowsing for people who know nothing about it and helpful for people who know a little too. Easy to read and informative"

Unlock Your Life With Pendulum Dowsing Books & MP3 Audios by Dean Fraser

DOWSING POCKETBOOKS

Book One – Anyone Can Dowse

Book Two – Pendulum Dowsing & Spiritual Healing

Book Three – Pendulum Dowsing & Crystal Healing

AUDIO BOOKS

Book One – Anyone Can Dowse

Books Two – Spiritual Healing

Unlock Your Life With Pendulum Dowsing

The Pocketbook
Based on full size paperback Anyone Can Dowse

Dean Fraser

First published in 1998

Pocketbook Edition Copyright © Dean Fraser 2018
Published by Alive to Thrive Ltd

Dean Fraser has asserted his right under the Copyright, Designs and Patents Act 1988 to be identified as the author of this book and work.

All rights reserved. No part of this publication may be reproduced, stored in a retrieval system or transmitted in any form or by any means, electronic, photocopying, recording or otherwise, without the prior permission of the copyright owner.

ISBN 978-1508617167

The information in this book should most definitely NOT be regarded as a substitute for medical treatment or counselling. If you are ill always seek professional medical advice. No claims medical or otherwise are made with regards the contents of this book.

Contents

Introducing Dowsing 07
Why Pendulum Dowsing? 11
What Exactly Is A Pendulum? 14
Getting Started 18
Getting The Most From Dowsing 27
Dowsing The Landscape 42
Dowsing For Health 49
Dowsing And Spirituality 54
Remaining Impartial 56
What Next 58
So, What Exactly Is Dowsing Then? 61

For all the people, past, present and future (now) who have inspired and helped me. You know who you are!

All photos and illustrations copyright of the author.

Introducing Dowsing

You will more than likely have seen traditional dowsers in books, on television or the internet, working away with their dowsing rods or hazel twig looking for water. Their rods or twig react when they find water by twitching or moving in various different directions. This is clearly extremely useful in drought areas or indeed for farmers who need to water their crops.

This book will aim to show that dowsing with a pendulum has far and more varied practical uses, limited perhaps only by our own imagination. We will see why a pendulum can be applied for amongst other applications - choosing vitamins and minerals, testing food and drink, finding lost articles, psychic development, discovering where to go on holiday or the perfect location to live, gold or oil prospecting, to answer virtually any question or unravel the truth. Also, to find water if that is what you want…

The power and potential of dowsing should never be underestimated, there are also several individuals who make an extremely good living working as professional dowsers offering their services to oil and mineral prospecting companies. These people tend to not shout about their discoveries or seek publicity, they don't really need to, already being well known to those who call on their services. Mainstream science has traditionally frowned upon dowsing as not being scientifically provable (although paradoxically there are some open-minded scientists who do dowse) these professional oil and mineral dowsers are in constant demand.

This book was first written in 1998 (going on to sell over 10,000 copies) and I decided it was time to update and make it available once mor in 2016. The copy your hold in your hands was updated from the original manuscript as a special Anniversary Edition to celebrate eighteen years since it first came out. I have ensured I keep the spirit and essence of the original book untouched and intact; adding only my own extra insights gained from experiences over the intervening years of showing so many how to dowse. If these experiences have taught me anything it is that dowsing can be amazing, enlightening, sometimes frustrating because it does have a habit of not always giving you the answer you hoped for, and occasionally even downright spooky when the illogical insight gained suddenly manifests in life in a very unexpected way.

I come from a long line of dowsers; my late uncle was for many years the trusted person in his drought ridden Essex village for finding water for the local farmers. He would use his rods or hazel twig and almost never failed to find water for the grateful farmer or landowner. Sometimes the water sitting many metres below the ground, nevertheless he still usually found it.

In teaching people to dowse I always feel I am giving them the keys to a better understanding of themselves and the World around them. I still get excited with them the first time it works and share a renewed awe for this unexplainable phenomenon.

Why Pendulum Dowsing?

There are still many dowsers who far prefer to dowse using rods or twigs and would never even consider dowsing with a pendulum, obviously there is nothing wrong with that, what I am seeking to demonstrate in this book is that a pendulum can be infinitely easier to work with in many situations where any other method would be more or less impossible.

Pendulums are by their very nature highly portable, they easily fit into a pocket or small bag and can be taken out to use as needed, then stowed away again until next time.

If you need to dowse discretely, without attracting unwanted attention, this is far easier with a pendulum. Rather than getting out your rods or hazel twig and expecting nobody else to notice!

The rod or twig dowser does tend to attract an interested crowd, waiting with bated breath to see the "wizard" in action. This is not always desirable, especially if you are in your local supermarket wishing to choose a healthy lunch and want a little help from your pendulum in deciding.

While I am still being "down" on rod or twig dowsers, another point to bear in mind is that their tools are rather susceptible to the wind blowing them in all directions. Having stood in a windy field with a good friend attempting to rod dowse an ancient long-barrow and with his rods constantly being blown to the left I can vouch for this one. A pendulum can be used in situations of pretty much any weather and still give a consistent response, as I will show later.

Before any traditional rod or twig dowsers throw this book down in disgust, I should say that I do also on occasions use rods and find them just as enlightening and exciting as a pendulum. Just not always quite as practical in my own personal experience. My pendulum usually travels in my pocket; a hazel twig couldn't be quite as easily carried upon my person.

What Exactly is a Pendulum?

A pendulum is simply some kind of weight that is in balance, suspended from a cord or chain, meaning it hangs perfectly weighted and centred. There are many options we can go for when choosing which pendulum to buy. There are shop or e-shop bought pendulums which can have been manufactured out of crystal, brass, steel or indeed any another metal, polished semi-precious stone of almost every conceivable type and wood.

Another way to go is to make your own pendulum. More or less any weighty object, such as a heavy gauge washer, an old-fashioned door key or even a plumb bob (obtainable from any DIY centre) suspended from a piece of thread or cord can make an excellent pendulum, with the added benefit of having being created by you.

I have two pendulums. My original one, from way back when, which is pure faceted crystal on a silver chain, this is used for personal dowsing and then another beautiful large pendulum made from polished reclaimed wood rather in the shape of a long plumb bob and this is saved for using in demonstrating dowsing to others as it does move in quite a dramatic and easily followed way. My slightly battered crystal pendulum only I can handle then it just carries my personal vibrations, and the wooden one can be held by anyone else who I happen to be demonstrating dowsing to.

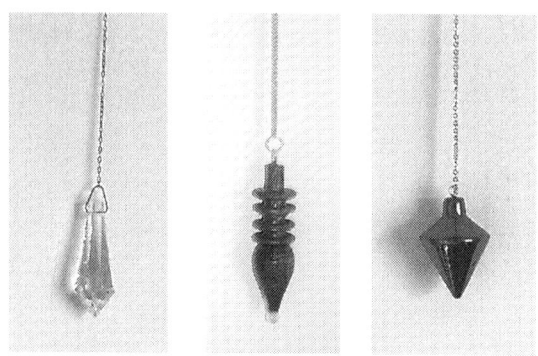

The author's well used crystal and reclaimed wood pendulums, plus a pure hematite gemstone pendulum

Bringing us rather conveniently to another important part of owning a pendulum you need to know about. Your pendulum needs to be protected from outside influences and the vibrations of others, at least when you are first starting out with learning how to dowse. My suggestion would be to acquire a small pouch the right size to place your pendulum in when you are not using it. If you have bought a pendulum from a retailer the chances are it may already come complete with a storage pouch. If not, it is likely that the retailer will stock them or alternatively if you are handy with a needle and thread you can always make your own. Do not use a silk pouch, as silk can generate an etheric charge of itself and may influence your pendulum. Cotton or some other natural fabric is best.

Over time your dowsing pendulum will gradually become attuned to your own essence and vibration. It will become very much your pendulum. Some dowsers feel fine and okay with letting others handle their pendulum, my advice would be to go with your gut instinct and act accordingly if someone wants to have a go with your pendulum. I believe you will know if the person in question if someone you feel will handle your pendulum with due respect.

Sometimes I find myself in a situation where I absolutely need to dowse for something, but inconveniently I do not have my pendulum with me. In this case I simply use my car key! I hold the key ring fob and let the key dangle down and act as the pendulum. This may not bring me the most dramatic dowsing response like my real pendulum, checking my results later though generally proves that it is still pretty accurate.

Getting Started

The art of dowsing with a pendulum is in reality remarkably simple and easy. It may sound more than a little complicated when described, however, once you are happily dowsing for yourself you will agree it really is simple and easy!

It is the interpreting of the results that can be a little more challenging sometimes…but more of that later, let's get back to basics first.

The way a pendulum works for everyone is by responding to specific questions asked of it in by moving in one of three different ways. The given answer can be Yes, No or Maybe. It shows us one of these answers every time we ask a question and it does this by moving in a particular direction in response to the question, giving the answer.

The movement a pendulum makes to answer a question can vary from person to person, and can include clockwise or counter-clockwise rotation, forward and backward rocking, side to side rocking, diagonal rocking or even shaking. Do not concern yourself with all these variations, the important movements are the ones that you yourself get. There is no right or wrong here.

Now You're Dowsing

Find somewhere quiet to sit where there is no chance of you being disturbed. A place far away from everyday distractions such as children, partners, televisions, radios, computers, phones or any of the other thousand and one things that could spoil your concentration. At this very first attempt at dowsing my suggestion would be not to mention to anyone else that you are going to be learning to dowse. Other people's comments, however well intentioned, could subconsciously influence your responses and you want your dowsing to be pure right from the start. Once you have quickly mastered dowsing by all means give demonstrations to family and friends, for now though privacy works better. Shhh!

As I mentioned, what you need to establish is which particular pendulum movement you are experiencing means to you. In your peaceful retreat, far from distractions, start to relax and clear your mind of all the thoughts that are running through it. Leave the mundane World behind, you are about to discover something magical and wonderful.

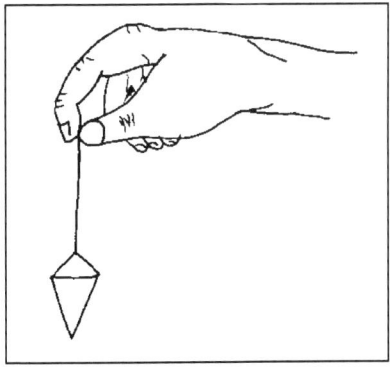

Take your pendulum in the hand you write with. Hold it by pinching the chain or cord between your thumb and forefinger, allowing about 15cm (6 inches) to hang freely before reaching the pendulum (you don't need to measure this, by the way, just approximately will be fine!), wrap any remaining length of cord inside your hand.

Say aloud or in your head, while concentrating "what is my Yes response?" the pendulum will now start to slowly vibrate and then gently at first move in a specific direction. Be patient as this can take a few seconds to start with. This can also seem a little eerie at first, as the pendulum slowly but surely starts to swing of its own accord and takes on a definite direction. This particular movement direction will now always be your Yes answer to any question you may ask your pendulum.

Having established your Yes response, the next useful answer you will clearly need is "what is my No response?"

This is done in exactly the same way - ask the question out loud or in your head and slowly the pendulum will take on a movement in a particular direction, but different from your Yes direction. Once it is moving nicely and surely you will have your established No response to any question you may ask of your pendulum.

Now by using your pendulum to ask questions you will be able to establish a definite Yes or No answer.

That is not all though. What happens if a question you ask does not have a readily available or obvious Yes or No response answer?

As an example of this, I mentioned earlier in the book it is possible to test food in order to establish if we should consume it or not and as promised we will go into this in more detail a little later on, for now though a little demonstration of how a pendulum can respond in a very literal way to a question.

We are in a cake shop and having taken a fancy to a lovely double chocolate fudge cake with extra cream, we might decide to use our pendulum to see if it is something we should eat. So, we ask the question of our pendulum "is this double chocolate fudge cake with extra cream something I should eat?" and get no response at all from the pendulum. Nothing happening whatsoever.

It cannot answer the question because you have not phrased the question correctly. You need to rephrase it according to what you want to know. "Is this cake safe for me to eat" may well get a Yes response. "Is this cake healthy for me to eat?" would probably be more likely to get a resounding No! Apologies to any cake makers reading this or chocoholics if I gave you cravings!

In my defence I am quite partial to a little vegan cake myself occasionally and dowsing can indeed be very literal…

Clearly what is needed is a response from your pendulum telling you that you either need to ask the question differently or whatever you are asking cannot be answered at this time. This does happen from time to time and my theory is that there are certain experiences we need to grow from and if we were forewarned by dowsing, we might avoid something we will learn from.

What we need then is a Maybe response. Enabling us to ask again in a different way for a definite Yes or No response or simply accept some things we are not yet meant to know.

The process is exactly the same as with when you established your Yes and No responses. Ask out loud or to yourself "what is my Maybe response?" Once again, your pendulum will take on a movement, different from your Yes and No, and this will then always be your Maybe response.

Once you have completed these exercises you will have all you need to get started with dowsing. You have your Yes, No or Maybe response to any question you care to ask and your pendulum will always give you one of the three answers. As we have learned, the art is in phrasing the questions to get the best possible use out of our pendulum. Remember pendulums will always work in a rather literal way; it is up to us to interpret the answers we get within the context of our own lives and what they mean to us.

Getting the Most from Dowsing

There are so many fascinating and illuminating ways in which we can integrate dowsing into our everyday lives. I am going to suggest a few examples and then pass on your dowsing future over to you, the best way we can learn is by our own personal experiences. Trust intuition and it will guide you in the right direction for you.

Testing Food and Drink

We did cover this briefly earlier in the book, here as promised is the bigger picture on how dowsing can help us to make correct choices about what to eat and drink. Before I start this section a word of warning – never eat anything past its use by date, even if dowsing says it is ok, also if something visually looks like it has gone off and the smell confirms this, the best thing to do is avoid eating it!

As we now know our pendulum can give us one of three responses to any question, Yes, No or Maybe. The art in testing food and drink using our pendulum is in knowing what it is we really want to know and asking the questions accordingly; as with our chocolate cake example of a few pages ago. We need to decide if we want to know if a particular food or drink is safe, healthy (or better still both) to consume.

A classic example of this would be with red wine. We could dowse to ask "is this safe to drink?" and get a Yes response. Further we could even ask "is this healthy to drink?" and still get the Yes response. If we don't ask the question "how much wine can I drink and still feel healthy, 1 glass? 2 glasses?" and so on until we get to a No answer, then we could still be in for a horrible hangover in the morning. It is quite possible that a moderate amount of quality organic wine can indeed be healthy for us; consuming 3 litres of this same wine of an evening could be anything but healthy! The art, as always, is in asking the correct question and patiently continuing until the answer is clear.

To test a food or drink we don't even need to have it there in front of us. If you have a good imagination and can vividly picture in your mind the item you wish to dowse for, you can ask your questions while holding the vision in your mind of the item.

If you struggle a little with bringing pictures into your mind and keeping that image fixed there, another way is to use a list of food or drink and a pencil. This can be especially useful when choosing from a menu in a restaurant or takeaway. Take the pencil and using the hand you don't write with, point to the different items down the list that interest you one by one and hold your pendulum in your usual dowsing hand and ask for the answers to the questions you have.

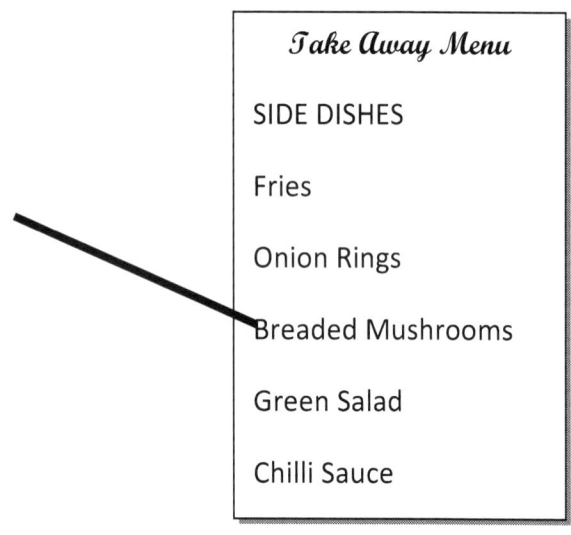

Remember when testing if food and drink is safe or healthy it is YOU that you are asking the pendulum to supply answers for. Do not assume that the same Yes, No or Maybe answers will apply to everyone else. If you are planning a dinner party it is always best to ask guests first if anyone has any food intolerances rather than risk serving them a lovely dish with traces of pecans and having to call an ambulance for your nut intolerant guest who is now turning an interesting shade of purple. Even when you dowsed and got a resounding Yes earlier the same evening when you asked if the dish was healthy, which of course it was for you…

Pendulums answer in a very literal way.

Further Using Lists in Dowsing

Lists enable us to narrow down choices, which is obviously especially useful. As we have already covered the "how to" part of dowsing a list, all I really need to add is that any kind of list can be dowsed. The possibilities are endless.

Decision Making – Blind Testing

We all face situations from time to time where it is difficult to know what to do for the best. The choices we face are confusing to us and even downright scary as we wonder what the outcome of our pondering and the subsequent choice we make will be.

Thankfully dowsing can be an excellent way of shedding a little insight into our decision making process and we can do this in a way that guarantees that our own subconscious thoughts or desires will not influence the response we get from our pendulum.

Whatever it is we have to literally decide about in all honesty hardly particularly matters in this process. It can be anything from what course to study at University, where to travel on holiday, if we should go on a certain date, where to live or any of the myriad of life-direction choices that crop up for everyone which requires some kind of action from us to resolve. Dowsing can be used to help practically whatever the subject.

You will need some A4 sized paper and a pencil for this exercise, and obviously your dowsing pendulum!

Tear the paper up into small pieces about 5x3cm. Those Virgo people who are reading can measure with a ruler and use scissors to cut them neatly until they are all identical, for the rest of us approximately 5x3cm is fine. just teasing, I do love Virgo people really (after all Virgo is my own ascendent star sign!). On each square write down one of the options you have in your decision making. I will use the example of someone who is undecided about which University course to apply for. Their choices could be from study medicine, archaeology, psychology, hairdressing or quantum physics. The University hopeful will write one of these options on each of the separate pieces of paper.

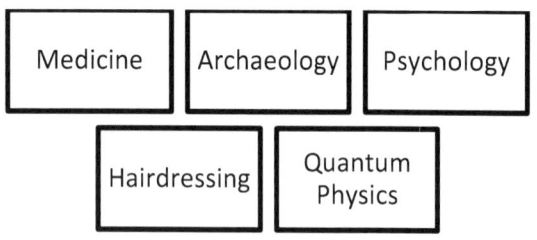

Turn the pieces of paper upside down, so the writing is face down. Did I mention that you should not be able to read the writing through the paper when it is face down? You shouldn't be able to. This is why we use a pencil rather than a pen.

Take your pendulum and one by one dowse over the papers asking something along the lines of "is this the best choice for me to make at this time?" again this can be out loud or in your head. You will get Yes, No or Maybe responses to each of the pieces of paper. The No ones can now be moved out of the way. Any Maybe response can be put to one side. If you have a definite Yes response over one particular piece of paper, now turn it over and see which option your blind testing with dowsing opted for.

If you do not have a definite Yes reply, but you do have a few Maybe responses, you can now also turn these over and see why it could be that you haven't got a definite Yes or No. You may need to ask further questions in order to come to a clearer conclusion.

There are some experiences we do need to go through; however bizarre they may seem at the time. Later it does usually tend to become clear exactly what it was all about. Dowsing makes it easier to get straight to the heart of the decision-making process and learn.

Prediction Using Dowsing

The one area where dowsing generally fails to provide useful answers is with gambling, which is a pity as I feel it would be really quite nice to win the national lottery every week, sadly it does not seem to work that way.

If you have a go at using dowsing to make your fortune picking lottery numbers or indeed with any other type of gambling, I wish the very best of luck to you, there have been many before you who have done the same and unfortunately had to carry on working for a living.

Is the future already decided? Can we accurately know what is in store for us? Perhaps. Then again would we really want to know what exactly is just around the corner?

My suggestion would be to use dowsing to look into the future in a very general sense. Dowsing in essence has to be enjoyable and why not have a bit of fun taking a bit of a peek into the possible future? The art is in asking the correct questions, then interpreting the answers in a way that makes sense within the context of your own life.

Asking about events in the future may make us change our mind about the direction our life is taking. Having said that I am a great believer in certain events occurring for our own greater good and our path of learning through life. So, the fact that you are now a dowser and are using your pendulum to get a glimpse of your own future could in fact well be the absolute perfect path for you to take in order to have certain experiences you would have never otherwise come across.

The Universe has a way of showing us the right path to tread and it looks like ours is one that integrates dowsing into our lives and the insights that having that power can bring. I love this paradox!

Finding Lost Articles

We can all misplace things and then expend needless energy and definitely needless stress on trying to find whatever the lost article is.

You will be pleased to know that the next time you cannot find your keys, phone, car, dog or whatever else you may have mislaid, then dowsing can help.

I will use the example of the last time I lost my mobile phone. Yes, I know I could just phone the number and follow the ring; however, on this occasion I knew it was switched off so that wasn't really much help.

Office	Dining Room/Kitchen	Utility *(Location of Phone)*
Lounge	Entrance Hall Stairs to 1st Floor	WC

Ground Floor

Bedroom	En-Suite Bathroom	Bedroom
Bedroom	Stairs from Ground Floor	Bathroom

1st Floor

I drew a rough floor plan of the rooms in my house and wrote down what each square shape on my plan represented in terms of located rooms on two levels. Next, I took my pendulum and trusty pencil, pointing in turn at each room and asking the question "is my phone in this room?" until I got my Yes reply. Then I was able to go to the right area of my house and facing in each direction of the room ask "is my phone in that part of the room?" until I narrowed it down and found it right there in the laundry basket in the utility room!

We can apply the same principal to any lost item in any place we think we may have lost it. If you think you have lost something on a journey, draw a rough map (or a really neat, detailed map if you prefer) of the route you have taken. Using your pencil, trace along the route asking out loud or in your head constantly "is my lost item here?" until you get the Yes response. Based on where you have discovered, you can then take appropriate action to hopefully recover whatever it was you misplaced.

Dowsing the Landscape

It doesn't matter if you are interested in finding lost treasure or an ancient Roman fort, dowsing can be used to find long hidden archaeology and in fact we do not even need to leave the comfort of our favourite chair if we do not wish to, although field work can be amazingly exciting.

All we need to decide is what it is we would like to actually find.

An Ordnance Survey Map of the area we are looking to explore is essential and our pendulum.

I am going to use as an example on how to find an ancient long-barrow (Neolithic burial chamber) which has long since vanished from obvious view within the landscape, although this can be applied to virtually anything you could be interested in locating both in the landscape or underground.

This is the same principal that the oil and mineral dowsers I mentioned in the introduction use in exploration; it works in precisely the same way.

When I personally did this exercise I was in the general location of what I was looking for, then I later set out on foot to explore and see if my dowsing findings made sense within what I could visually ascertain from the landscape.

The author in action near a church in Lancashire, England

Spreading out the OS map flat on the bonnet of my car (it was a nice still day, no wind) I firstly dowsed along the bottom edge of the map and asked "is the lost ancient long-barrow in a square upward of here?" and eventually got a Yes response. Then I went down the left-hand edge of the map to repeat the exercise, this time asking, "is the lost ancient long-barrow in a square to the right of here?" and I got my Yes response.

I can tell you for sure this is incredibly exciting when you are actually on location because then it was time to go along to the area my dowsing had found and see for myself. Sure enough there were clear indications in the particular field I was exploring that a long time ago there could well have been something there. Later I was able to confirm through some online research the existence of the long barrow, long since ploughed away by generations of farmers.

Use the same concept to search for anything that takes your interest. Like I mentioned, it is not actually necessary to leave your house if you do not want to, you could lay your map out on a table and dowse it in the comfort of your own home; although for me at least the thrill of becoming a landscape detective to search for long lost features is irresistible.

Our ancient ancestors could feel the landscape and the Earth energy or ley lines, using them to decide where to construct monuments in the landscape and bury their dead; ponds along energy or ley lines are where they made offerings to their deities.

Here in our "civilised" 21st century we have forgotten so much of the genetic heritage from our ancestors; most of us do not live in-tune with seasons as they did and most of us cannot read the landscape in the way that would have been perfectly second nature to them.

With practice and the help of our pendulum, we can train ourselves to be able to live, at least a little, as they would have done. Understanding our relationship to our beautiful planet and seeing the landscape as a living evolving entity, which we are all inter-connected with. Learning to respect nature and her mysteries is all part of starting to feel through our intuition. Getting to the point where we can know about energy in nature without actually needing to dowse at all, reading the landscape and trusting our inner knowledge.

Ley Lines

Archaeologist and businessman, Alfred Watkins is credited with coming up with the term Ley Line and his wonderful 1927 book The Ley Hunter's Manual still makes for interesting reading.

Ley Lines are a network of energy lines which travel sometimes great distances through the landscape, often connecting significant ancient sites. The theory is that our Neolithic and perhaps even earlier ancestors knew of Ley Lines and planned their spiritual areas to be located along established Ley Lines, forming an interconnection with themselves, the Earth, and their deities.

Using the same principle as in the previous section, it is possible to dowse for Ley Lines using OS maps. My suggestion is to firstly start with a well-known ancient site such as Stonehenge or Uluru (Ayers Rock) and dowse for yourself any Ley Lines running through or from these sites. Please avoid researching anyone else's discoveries beforehand, leave it until after your own dowsing and then by all means go on the internet to see if your findings match those of others.

There are some great online forums out there for exchanges of ideas and information. I shan't suggest any specific websites as such information dates incredibly quickly and this book will be in publication for many years.

Dowsing for Health

Doctors go to medical school to train for at least five years plus their vocational years of training in order to become qualified.

I obviously believe in the power of dowsing, having said that a little common sense is prudent here. I cannot possibly understand how the human body works in the same way a doctor would. Therefore, the dowser who is attempting to diagnose a condition in someone, without the benefit of medical training, cannot know what is really going on with their illness and where their symptoms are originating from. The art, as always, is in knowing the correct questions to ask, without medical training this is impossible. A doctor clearly does know the right questions, they are able to test using cutting-edge technology and then makes a diagnosis based on complete knowledge of sympathetic symptoms together with the learned expertise in interpreting them.

Surely the utopia here would be to find a medically qualified doctor who is also able to look at his or her patients in a holistic sense? Rather than automatically prescribing drugs, they would look into the much wider potential causes of the complaint such as emotional balance, stress, environmental factors or indeed the lifestyle of their patient and only then make their recommendations based on the complete picture of their patient that emerges.

Such holistic medical doctors do exist. They are just a little thin on the ground, especially here in the UK. This is where the internet comes in incredibly useful. If I had something afflicting me I would consider that it was worth travelling to see such a practitioner, and I would be secure in the knowledge that here I am being treated by someone who understands the whole of a person, rather than only how their body functions.

There are some wonderful doctors out there who are saving lives every day and if I had an accident, I would certainly want taking to one straight away. If I were unfortunate enough to develop an illness, however, and I had the choice to make, I would personally go to consult a holistic medically qualified doctor.

My advice is never to gamble with your health, if you feel ill seek professional medical attention. Dowsing should never be used to self-diagnose or diagnose anyone else (unless you are actually a qualified doctor and even then, check your results conventionally please before treating your patient!).

Vitamins *(based upon a section from The Magic of Holistic Living by Dean Fraser)*

We all have easy access to just about every and any type of possible vitamin, mineral or supplement conceived of or imagined. All we have to do is hit the high street or click a mouse. Yet how many of these vits do we genuinely need to be taking and how many simply pass through our bodies serving little useful purpose?

The message here is, vits are easily obtainable and we can all self-diagnose. If you do genuinely feel that you could use some extra vitamins over and above your usual diet, take the time to go and get checked out by a health professional.

Then you're going to ensure you're supplementing with something you actually need short term.

If you are veggie or vegan, it's almost mandatory to have your B vits checked periodically as a matter of course and for peace of mind. A nicely balanced diet might well leave further supplementation obsolete. The other thing to bear in mind here is that our needs are more than likely going to be entirely different during the summer months as opposed to winter; again if your instinct is suggesting you would benefit from supplementation, a visit to your GP or another kind of healthcare professional allows you to know for sure. Facts when it comes to our wellbeing are always preferable to guesswork.

If you decide after that you are going to dowse for any potential vitamins or minerals you feel might be lacking in your diet, by all means go ahead and do it, ensuring later to have your results verified by your chosen healthcare professional.

Dowsing and Spirituality

I am sure you will find a great deal many more uses for dowsing than the few we have started off with here or even that I can possibly think of. Dowsing can be amazingly useful on an everyday basis, providing a short-cut through thought processes and sometimes illuminating the choices we have to make in a completely different way than we first imagined possible. It is also highly personal and you will find the ideal way to integrate dowsing into your life and lifestyle.

My belief is that the forces that govern our Universe and in indeed our own higher selves, only allows such knowledge that we are currently evolved enough to comprehend to come into our sphere of activity. If our consciousness is not ready to take on certain wisdoms then we will not be able to obtain them.

If we are dowsing to have a peep into the future and if we persist with a certain line of questioning, continually getting the Maybe response from our pendulum, then whatever we are seeking to know is not for us at this time.

Evolvement comes from living, making mistakes which are not really mistakes but learning, walking our talk and sometimes tripping up along the way a few times before we finally get the message about what we need in order to grow. Shedding old patterns of behaviour as we progress through life, rather like the snake sheds its own skin to renew itself.

Knowing more about ourselves and our interconnectedness with all things is the start of true wisdom. If we choose to attempt to grow, we have a great tool to help us, our dowsing pendulum.

Remaining Impartial

One of the greatest challenges to anyone in dowsing is to overcome our own subconscious wishes or desires from being allowed to impinge upon the results we obtain from our pendulum.

An example of this would be if we are looking to make a particular career choice and in our minds eye the new job seems rather a scary prospect, in terms of perhaps having to learn completely new skills or leave an established comfort zone; and yet the long-term rewards personally and financially are going to be immeasurable.

Taking your pendulum and asking "is this job one I should take" you find you get the No response. You think "Oh good, then I should stay right where I am then and not taking the risk, problem solved".

Right?

Nope!

The chances are your own subconscious fears affected the outcome of the dowsing.

So how are we to overcome our own thoughts influencing results and remain impartial?

One way is to use the blind testing method from a few pages back. Another is to ask someone else who dowses, who you trust, to test for you and see what answers they get compared to your own.

The same goes for testing food and drink. Stay as balanced and centred within yourself as possible. Not caring too much about the responses you will get, but rather wanting to seek the truth and only the truth.

This is a good lesson…remain as detached as possible from the likely response from your pendulum, by all means be passionate about your dowsing, however, staying in an impartial emotional state when asking your questions of your pendulum.

What Next?

For me dowsing is all about developing an inner link to our spiritual self and learning to trust what has been called our intuition or gut instinct.

Our dowsing pendulum is the perfect tool for guiding us, nurturing our intuition and having the confidence to go with those choices which feel right deep inside.

The next statement might seem a little shocking, given the premise of this book to promote and popularize pendulum dowsing to as many as possible.

"It is entirely possible and perhaps even desirable to get to the point where it is unnecessary to even use a pendulum when dowsing!" Dean Fraser

Okay, this might well be a long, long way down the line, however, the concept does hold true. If dowsing is actively developed and practised, there definitely comes a time when the responses can be felt in your fingers or even just forefinger. Although it can still be pleasant and reassuring to hold your pendulum, the essence of the dowsing response is felt pretty much independently of the pendulum movement. This level of heightened intuition won't happen in all cases, the author does know of a small number of dowsers who use their forefinger rather than a pendulum and feel the different responses instinctively, knowing exactly what they mean.

In my third decade of dowsing I do occasionally eschew my pendulum when seeking answers, to usually fall back on it just to validate my findings at this stage in my evolvement – they generally prove to be correct. This is something I occasionally demonstrate just for fun in my classes, if I am feeling particularly spiritually connected, yet there is a serious thought behind it, to show possibilities to my students.

We are all here to grow…only expectation brings success.

So, What Exactly is Dowsing Then?

And now my esteemed readers we come to that great unanswered question "so what exactly is dowsing?"

Oh, do you want me to tell you the answer?

Sorry…not got an idea! Well, okay I do have a few ideas, yet like anyone else my guess is as good as yours.

What dowsing isn't is perhaps easier to answer – it isn't a parlour game or trick; it isn't infallible and it certainly isn't an excuse to opt out of making decisions. Our pendulum shows a possible course of action, the final decision is still ours to make if we go with the answer or something else.

Many theories exist as to where the answers in dowsing come from.

Is it coming from the etheric field of the Earth?

Perhaps ley lines are involved?

Is it entities from the spirit world helping us in this?

Do the answers come from our own auras and are then transmitted through our fingers?

Our higher selves or soul?

Angels?

Aliens perhaps?

My own theory is that to dowse is to be partially attuned to another aspect of ourselves – call it spirit, soul or higher self. That part of us that exists on a higher level than our third dimensional physical bodies alone. Our pendulum offers a short-cut way of communicating with our own spiritual self, is my theory.

Whatever the truth, we can be said to be literally helping ourselves when we dowse.

Perhaps you will be the one who will finally solve the riddle and prove beyond any doubt where the answers in dowsing are coming from?

I wish you all joyous discoveries and harmonious insights!

"The only way to awaken all the dormant magic within is to feel grateful that we have already unlocked it. I adore this apparent paradox" - Dean Fraser

ABOUT DEAN FRASER

More of less from birth Dean Fraser knew there existed far more than the three dimensions most of us take for granted. Since his infant years he had been offering healings; and having already experienced his fair share of personal growth opportunities (some might label them challenges...) by the late 1980's Dean resolved to undertake a personal quest for metaphysical growth. This ongoing journey has seen him read thousands of books, travel across two continents in search of truths, network with fellow seekers of enlightenment through sharing wisdoms collectively, and personally visit countless sacred sites to attune with their energies. Over the last three decades Dean has become one of the world's leading advocates of dowsing as a means of connecting to our own intuition, also a passionate teacher of meditation and holistic lifestyles. Alongside poetry he found another channel for spiritual expression through intuitive art as a creative outlet. Dean's calls his transcendent paintings Beyond Art. They have gained a reputation for acting as a powerful focus for meditation and to raise the chi or positive vibrational energy in any room. Dean Fraser tours globally sharing life-affirming stories and poetry.

DOWSING, GHOSTS & PSYCHIC HEALING

TRUE STORIES FROM THE CASEBOOK OF A METAPHYSICIAN

Dean Fraser

Bestselling author of the Unlock Your Life With Pendulum Dowsing series of books

THE POCKETBOOK

Unlock Your Life With Pendulum Dowsing

Crystal Healing

DEAN FRASER

Pocketbook Edition of Book Three in the series

www.deanfrasercentral.com

Printed in Great Britain
by Amazon